MEN...

Can't Live With Them,
Can't Live *With* Them.

Tania Golightly

SUMMERSDALE

Summersdale Publishers Ltd
46 West Street
Chichester
West Sussex
PO19 1RP
England

ISBN 1 84024 052 0

A CIP catalogue record for this book is available from the British Library.

Printed and bound in Great Britain.

In olden times a stupid man who didn't do
anything was called a gentleman.

Now he's called a boyfriend.

What's the difference
between a man and E.T.?

E.T. phoned home.

What do you get when you cross
a stupid man with a pig?

Nothing.
There are some things even a pig won't do.

How can you tell if a man
is going to be unfaithful?

He's breathing.

My doctor's so stupid that if he can't
cure you, he just touches up the X-rays.

Definition of a stupid man —

someone who walks into an antique shop
and asks 'what's new'?

What's the difference between
a pub and a G-spot?

A man can usually find the pub.

Having sex with your husband is like getting
an injection at the doctor's.

It's all over before you feel a thing.

What happened to the man who
cleaned his ears out?

His head caved in.

My man has the brain
of a four-year-old boy . . .
and I bet he was glad
to get rid of it.

My boyfriend is a flower child —

he's a blooming idiot.

My husband took the dog to obedience school.

The dog got a higher mark than he did.

Her: Can you think on your feet?

Him: Of course. Who else's
feet would I think on?

I knew a man who was so stupid
he thought Shirley Temple
was a children's synagogue.

A stupid man heard that a
comet was a star with a tail.

He now thinks Lassie is a speeding planet.

He's so stupid, at nursery school
he failed the sandpit.

My husband has a terrible
inferiority complex . . .

and he's right.

My boyfriend's so hopeless he
gets junk mail that starts,

'You may already be a loser . . .'

My boyfriend's so unpopular
even the Samaritans hung up on him.

My husband's head is so big
his ears have different postcodes.

I know a man who is so big-headed
when he prays he says,

'Dear God, do you need anything?'

My husband has two main problems —

he thinks everyone else is better than him . . .

and so do they.

My husband is very proud of our lawn.

Every blade of grass
is exactly three feet high.

Why can't men find the G-spot?

Because they hate asking for directions.

My husband and I were
happy for fifteen years . . .

then we met each other.

What is a man's idea of doing the cooking?

Phoning the pizza delivery company.

Why do men play dumb all the time?

Who says they're playing?

What's the difference between
a husband and a lover?

Day and night.

What is a husband?

Someone who stands by his wife
in troubles she would never have
had if she hadn't married him
in the first place.

To have more than one wife is bigamy.

To have more than one
husband is just insanity.

Everything you need to know about a man
you will find in his pants drawer.

How do you know a man
has cooked the dinner?

The salad's burnt.

Why do men's hearts make
the best transplants?

They're never used.

How can you tell if a
man is cheating on you?

He has a bath more than once a month.

What do you get if you cross
a man with a gorilla?

A really stupid gorilla.

What is a man's idea of
a sophisticated cocktail?

An olive in a glass of beer.

Sex is like bridge.

If you have a good hand
you don't need a partner.

What is a man's most effective
form of contraceptive?

His personality.

How can you tell if your
man is really stupid?

He tries to work out which
wine goes best with lager.

Why don't men get brain disease?

Germs don't grow in a vacuum.

My boyfriend's so stupid he had a thought
once but it died of loneliness.

What's the difference between
a man and a parrot?

At least you can have a
conversation with a parrot.

Why did God make man?

She forgot to put legs on snakes.

What's the difference between a
man and an untidy desk?

You can sort out an untidy desk.

My man's so stupid he thinks
Sherlock Holmes is a housing estate.

My man uses his head a lot . . .

if you look closely you can see the dents.

Why did the stupid man use his head?

He felt like having a new experience.

My man's so stupid
he can't even spell I.Q.

My man is the only person I know
who can misspell his initials.

I know a man who was so stupid he couldn't
have a battle of wits with anyone.

He only had enough ammunition
for a small skirmish.

My husband looks like an intelligent guy
but that's the only impersonation he does.

When they were giving out brains
my man was the first in line —

he just held the door open for everyone else.

A stupid man donated his brain to
science but they gave it back.

My man had a really great thought . . .

but then he sat down and squashed it.

What do you call a man who complains all day,
watches football all night and farts in bed?

Average.

What, to a man, is a
long-term relationship?

A second date.

Why don't men make ice-cubes?

They can't find the recipe.

It may have been a man who
invented the toilet seat . . .

but it was a woman who
thought of putting a hole in it.

If it has tyres or testicles,
it'll be trouble.

Talking to a man is like
polishing a wok —

you can work at it for days
but what's the point?

Why are men so unhappy
with being men?

There's so little chance
of advancement.

What is a man's favourite hobby?

Collecting dust.

How does a stupid man
get most of his exercise?

By jumping to conclusions.

He was so stupid, he wanted
to become a farmer . . .

so he studied pharmacy.

How do you get rid of
unwanted, excess fat?

Divorce him.

What was the first thing
Adam said to Eve?

"Stand back, I don't know
how big this thing gets!"

What's the difference between
a man and a good book?

You can get some pleasure out of a book.

I never forget a face —

I can remember both of his.

My man is an artist —

he draws flies.

How do you know
if your man is into hygiene?

He changes his underwear once a month
whether he needs to or not.

I wouldn't say he smells
but if he stays in one room
for too long the police start
looking for the dead body.

My man's hair is soft and fluffy —

just like his head.

His nose is so big he can
smell into the future.

My husband's so ugly
the children use his face as a doorstop.

My man's such a weakling
he needs two assistants
to help him change his mind.

How is a stupid man like herpes?

You can't get rid of
either once you've got them.

Why do stupid men only
get half-hour lunch breaks?

So their bosses don't have
to retrain them.

What won't a stupid man stand for?

A woman on the bus.

How is a stupid man like the
local council complaints office?

Both are impossible to get through to
when you need to talk.

What is a stupid man's
definition of boxer shorts?

Fallout.

How is a stupid man
like a set of car keys?

Both are easily mislaid.

What is a stupid man's
favourite thought of the day?

Look up a friend.

What's the similarity
between men and beer bottles?

They're both empty from the neck up.

What is the difference between men and pigs?

Pigs don't turn into men when they drink.

How are men like noodles?

They're always in hot water and they lack taste.

Why do men like BMWs?

Because they can spell it.

Why are cans of beer easy to open?

Look who's opening them.

What did God say
after she created man?

I can do better.

How can you tell
if your man's a loser?

Even the Samaritans hang up on him.

What's the difference
between men and alley cats?

Men don't know how to wash themselves.

Men divide into two main types —

studs and duds.

What's the hardest thing
to teach a man?

How to operate a laundry basket.

My man's so stupid
he thinks intercourse
is a racetrack.

My man's so stupid he thinks
the erogenous zones
are somewhere near the equator.

How do you define a talented man?

One who can dribble out of both sides
of his mouth at the same time.

Why do men have belly-buttons?

So they've got somewhere
to put their chewing gum.

Did you hear about the bloke who
broke his leg playing golf?

He fell off the ball wash.

Did you hear about the
stupid man who went skydiving?

He missed earth.

How do you know that
a woman is in love?

She divorces her husband.

There is only one thing that keeps
most women from being happily married:

their husbands.

What do men mean when they say
they like simple foods?

They mean they like food in
easy-to-open packages.

How do you get rid
of a pain in the neck?

You divorce him.

When is the safest time for sex?

When your boyfriend's away.

If it's true that eight out of ten men
write with a ball-point pen,
what do the other two do with it?

Support men's lib —

burn his Y-fronts.

My man's bisexual —

he never knows whether
he's coming or going.

What's the only sure way of
getting something
hard between your legs?

Buying a motorbike.

How many men does it
take to tile a bathroom?

It depends how thinly you slice them.

What do men and dog-poo
have in common?

The older they get the easier
they are to pick up.

How do you know if your
boyfriend's bad in bed?

He gives up sex for Lent
and you don't notice until Easter.

My boyfriend's so bad in bed
that when they see him even
prostitutes have a headache.

Why are men like popcorn?

They satisfy you, but only for a little while.

Why is food better than men?

Because you don't have to
wait an hour for seconds.

What's the difference
between men and dogs?

Men don't hump
women's legs at parties.

How do you make a man
laugh on a Monday?

Tell him a joke on Friday.

What do you call a spot
on a man's bum?

A brain tumour.

How do you give a man
a quick brain transplant?

Blow in his ear.

Why is it dangerous for men
to eat pickled onions?

Because their heads get stuck in the jars.

Why should men get washed
in the kitchen sink?

Because that's where you wash vegetables.

How do you put a sparkle in a man's eyes?

Shine a torch in his ears.

Man: I only know how to cook two things —
steak and fried eggs.

Woman: Great, which one is this?

Other Humour Books from Summersdale

More Chat-up Lines and Put Downs
Stewart Ferris   £3.99

How To Chat-up Women (Pocket edition)
Stewart Ferris   £3.99

How To Chat-up Men (Pocket edition)
Kitty Malone   £3.99

Enormous Boobs
The Greatest Mistakes In The History of the World
Stewart Ferris   £4.99

101 Uses for a Losing Lottery Ticket
Shovel/Nadler   £3.99

Girl Power
Kitty Malone   £3.99

The Kama Sutra For One
O'Nan and P. Palm   £3.99

101 Reasons Not To Do Anything
*A Collection of Cynical
and Defeatist Quotations*   £3.99

A Little Bathroom Book £3.99

Available from all good bookshops.